ALL ABOUT ANIMALS IN THE SNOW

All About Arctic Foxes

Kerrily Sapet

EZ READERS
AN IMPRINT OF
MITCHELL LANE PUBLISHERS

CREATING YOUNG NONFICTION READERS

EZ Readers offer nonfiction for beginning readers in PreK through first grade, using simple language, clear illustrations, and engaging facts to build vocabulary and confidence.

TIPS FOR READING NONFICTION WITH BEGINNING READERS

Talk about Nonfiction

Begin by explaining that nonfiction books give us information that is true. The book will be organized around a specific topic or idea, and we may learn new facts through reading.

Look at the Parts

Most nonfiction books have helpful features. Our *EZ Readers* include color photographs and graphic aids, a table of contents, a glossary, and an index. Share the purpose of these features with your reader.

Color Photos and Graphic Aids

A lot of information can be found by "reading" photos, charts, maps, and other graphic aids found within nonfiction texts. Help your reader learn more about the different ways information can be displayed.

Table of Contents

Located at the front of the book, this list shows the big ideas within the text and the page numbers where they can be found.

Glossary

Located at the back of the book, the glossary defines key words and phrases that are related to the topic. These words and phrases can be found in the text in colored type.

Index

Located at the back of the book, an index is an alphabetical list of topics and the page numbers where they can be found.

With a little help and guidance about reading nonfiction, you can feel good about introducing a young reader to the world of *EZ Readers* nonfiction books.

EZ Readers is an imprint of:

Mitchell Lane
PUBLISHERS

2001 SW 31st Avenue
Hallandale, FL 33009
mitchelllanepub.com

 Printed and bound in the United States of America.

First Edition, 2026.

Author: Kerrily Sapet
Editor: Morgan Brody

ISBN 979-8-89260-848-0 (library binding)
ISBN 979-8-90145-041-3 (paperback)
ISBN 979-8-89260-945-6 (ebook)

LC record available at https://lccn.loc.gov/2025950856

Photo credits: Adobe, Pixasquare, cover, 1, 2, 3, 4, 8, 12, 15,19, 21, 22, 23, 24; Adobe, Tukinoto, cover, 1; Shutterstock, Alexey Seafarer, cover, 1; Adobe, Julia, 3, 9, 10, 14, 18, 22; Shutterstock, LightField Studios, 5; Shutterstock, Alexey Seafarer, 6–7; Shutterstock, outdoorsman, 9; Shutterstock, Jiri Hrebicek, 10–11, 22; Shutterstock, Alexey Seafarer, 13, 22; Shutterstock, Ve Shandor, 14; Dreamstime, Pureimagination, 18, 22; Shutterstock, Holly S Cannon, 20; Shutterstock, ManoStudioArt, 21; Shutterstock, grayjay, 22; Shutterstock, Frank Fichtmueller, 22

Table of Contents

Meeting An Arctic Fox

Imagine you are walking in the winter. Snow crunches under your boots. The wind is freezing cold. Your coat keeps you warm.

An animal darts across the snow. It's the size of a large cat. An **arctic** fox! You almost didn't see it because its fur is white like the snow. Arctic foxes live in the coldest places on Earth.

Fox Watching

The fox has thick, warm fur. You see its dark eyes and small black nose. It has a long fluffy tail.

FASCINATING FOX!

Foxes wrap their tails around their bodies like blankets while sleeping.

FASCINATING FOX!

Some arctic fox dens have been used for over 300 years.

The fox disappears into a hole. It's gone into its **den**—a cozy underground home. Dens are like mazes. They have many tunnels and entrances.

You hear the fox. It sounds like a dog. Arctic foxes bark, growl, whine, and purr like cats. They make noises to **communicate**. They use sounds to warn of danger, find family members, or show they are happy or scared.

FASCINATING FOX!

Arctic foxes follow polar bears to eat their leftover food.

Looking for Food

You see the fox again. It pounces on a small animal. It caught a **lemming** to eat. Arctic foxes also eat birds and eggs.

Where Do Arctic Foxes Live?

Another fox pops out of the den. Arctic foxes travel in groups. A group of foxes is called a **skulk**. Some arctic foxes **migrate**. They travel hundreds of miles searching for food.

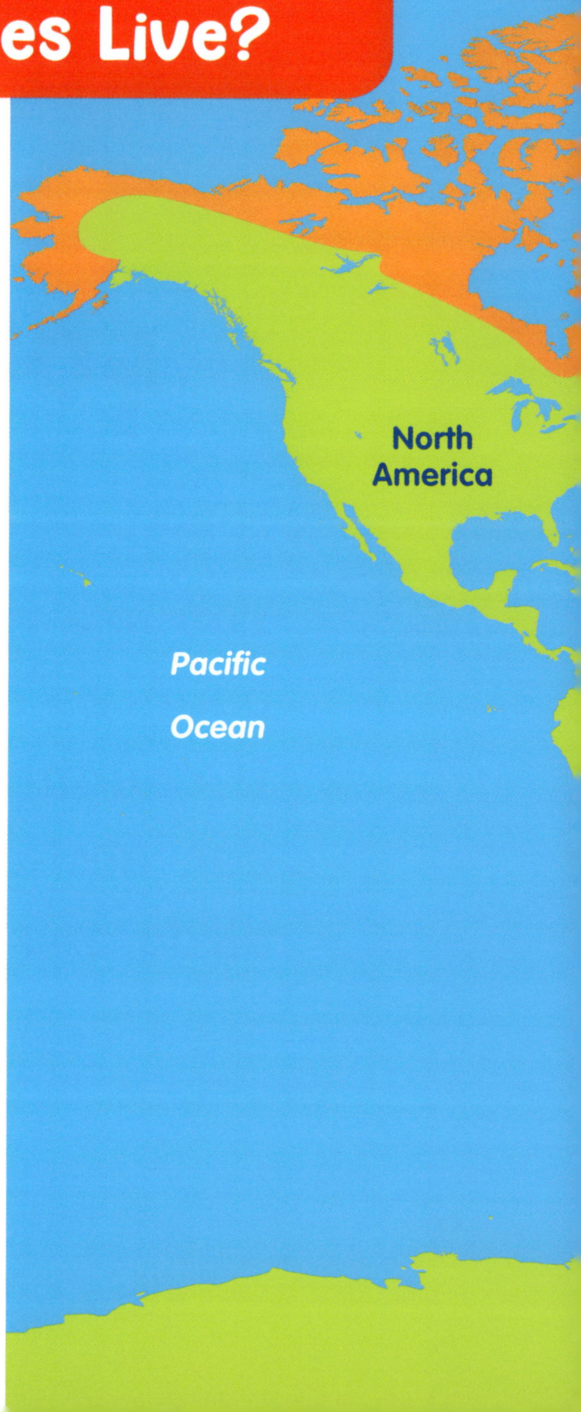

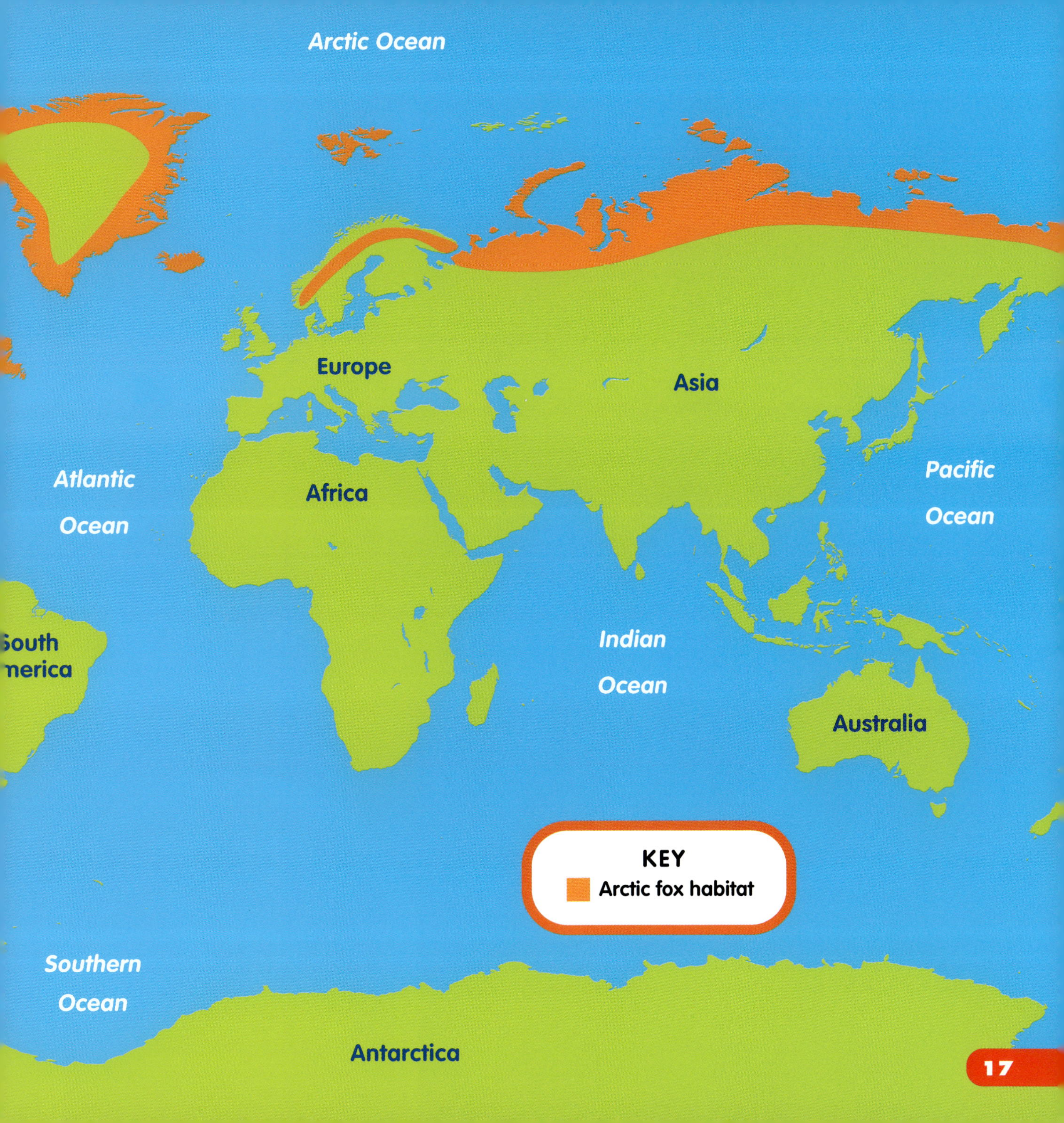

Arctic Ocean
Europe
Asia
Atlantic Ocean
Africa
Pacific Ocean
South America
Indian Ocean
Australia
KEY
Arctic fox habitat
Southern Ocean
Antarctica

FASCINATING FOX!

A mother can give birth to twelve **kits** at one time.

Arctic Fox Families and the Future

You hear baby foxes in the den. They are called kits. Kits are born blind and deaf. They are the size of a tennis ball. Both parents care for the kits.

Arctic foxes can live three to six years. They need the snow and ice on Earth to survive. Someday you might see a real arctic fox.

Parts of an Arctic Fox

Tail

Arctic foxes have long bushy tails. They help the fox stay warm.

Nose

Arctic foxes have small noses. They can smell a seal den from one mile away.

Ears

Arctic foxes have small, furry ears. They can hear lemmings moving under the snow.

Fur

Arctic foxes have thick white fur in winter to blend in with snow. Their fur turns darker in summer to match the land.

Feet

Arctic foxes have furry feet and toes. The fur keeps their feet warm and helps them grip the slippery ice.

Glossary

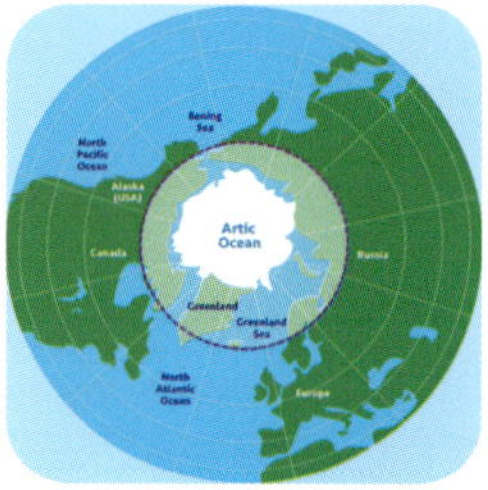

arctic (ARK-tik) a very cold place near the top of the Earth where there is lots of ice and snow

den (den) a safe place where an animal lives or rests

communicate (kuh-myoon-i-kayt) to share ideas or feelings by making sounds

kit (kit) a baby fox

lemming (LEM-ing) a furry animal that looks like a tiny mouse

migrate (my-GRAYT) when animals move to find food or warmer weather

skulk (SK-uhl-k) a group of foxes

Quiz

1. Do arctic foxes live in trees?

   A. Yes B. No

2. Do arctic foxes have warm fur?

   A. Yes B. No

3. Do arctic foxes eat polar bears?

   A. Yes B. No

4. Are arctic fox babies called kits?

   A. Yes B. No

ANSWER KEY DO NOT PEEK!

ANSWER KEY:

1. No
2. Yes
3. No
4. Yes

Further Reading

Blote, Mari. *Arctic Foxes.*
Mankato, MN: The Creative Company, 2025.

Koonoo, Brian. *Arctic Fox.*
Iqaluit, Nunavut: Inhabit Media, 2024.

Szymanski, Jennifer. *Arctic Animals.*
New York, NY: Scholastic, 2023.

On the Internet

Arctic Fox Facts for Kids

https://kids.nationalgeographic.com/animals/mammals/facts/arctic-fox

Read more and see pictures of arctic foxes.

Arctic Fox

https://www.pdza.org/animals/arctic-tundra/arctic-fox/

Meet the arctic foxes living at the Point Defiance Zoo & Aquarium.

Icelandic Arctic Fox

https://noisefromiceland.com/icelandic-arctic-fox/

Listen to the sounds arctic foxes make.

Index

About the Author

Kerrily Sapet has written more than 40 books for kids. She lives near Chicago with her family. Foxes are one of her favorite animals. Sometimes a red fox sleeps in the bushes behind her house. The fox has a thick bushy tail with a white tip. Sapet has never seen an arctic fox. She hopes to see one someday.